TEAM USA

THE ROAD TO THE
WORLD'S MOST POPULAR
CUP:

HISTORY OF THE CUP

MAKING THE FINAL 32

TEAM USA

TOP TEAMS

WORLD STARS

TEAM USA

Andrew Luke

MASON CREST

MASON CREST

450 Parkway Drive, Suite D I Broomall, Pennsylvania 19008
(866) MCP-BOOK (toll-free)

Andrew Luke

First printing
9 8 7 6 5 4 3 2 1

ISBN (hardback) 978-1-4222-3952-0
ISBN (series) 978-1-4222-3949-0
ISBN (ebook) 978-1-4222-7830-7

Cataloging-in-Publication Data on file
with the Library of Congress

QR CODES AND LINKS TO THIRD-PARTY CONTENT

You may gain access to certain third-party content ("Third-Party Sites") by scanning and using the QR Codes that appear in this publication (the "QR Codes"). We do not operate or control in any respect any information, products, or services on such Third-Party Sites linked to by us via the QR Codes included in this publication, and we assume no responsibility for any materials you may access using the QR Codes. Your use of the QR Codes may be subject to terms, limitations, or restrictions set forth in the applicable terms of use or otherwise established by the owners of the Third-Party Sites. Our linking to such Third-Party Sites via the QR Codes does not imply an endorsement or sponsorship of such Third-Party Sites or the information, products, or services offered on or through the Third-Party Sites, nor does it imply an endorsement or sponsorship of this publication by the owners of such Third-Party Sites.

CONTENTS

KEY ICONS TO LOOK FOR:

Words to Understand: These words with their easy-to-understand definitions will increase the reader's understanding of the text while building vocabulary skills.

Sidebars: This boxed material within the main text allows readers to build knowledge, gain insights, explore possibilities, and broaden their perspectives by weaving together additional information to provide realistic and holistic perspectives.

Educational videos: Readers can view videos by scanning our QR codes, providing them with additional educational content to supplement the text. Examples include news coverage, moments in history, speeches, iconic sports moments, and much more!

Text-Dependent Questions: These questions send the reader back to the text for more careful attention to the evidence presented there.

Research Projects: Readers are pointed toward areas of further inquiry connected to each chapter. Suggestions are provided for projects that encourage deeper research and analysis.

Series Glossary of Key Terms: This back-of-the book glossary contains terminology used throughout this series. Words found here increase the reader's ability to read and comprehend higher-level books and articles in this field.

Aggregate: combined score of matches between two teams in a two-match with each often referred to as "legs") format, typically with each team playing one home match.

Away goals rule: tie-breaker applied in some competitions with two-legged matches. In cases where the aggregate score is tied, the team that has scored more goals away from home is deemed the winner.

Cap: each appearance by a player for his national team is referred to as a cap, a reference to an old English tradition where players would all receive actual caps.

Challenge: common term for a tackle—the method of a player winning the ball from an opponent—executed when either running at, beside, or sliding at the opponent.

Clean sheet: referencing no marks being made on the score sheet, when a goalkeeper or team does not concede a single goal during a match; a shutout.

Derby: match between two, usually local, rivals; e.g., Chelsea and Arsenal, both of which play in London.

Dummy: skill move performed by a player receiving a pass from a teammate; the player receiving the ball will intentionally allow the ball to run by them to a teammate close by without touching it, momentarily confusing the opponent as to who is playing the ball.

Equalizer: goal that makes the score even or tied.

First touch: refers to the initial play on a ball received by a player.

Football: a widely used name for soccer. Can also refer to the ball.

Group of death: group in a cup competition that is unusually competitive because the number of strong teams in the group is greater than the number of qualifying places available for the next phase of the tournament.

Kit: soccer-specific clothing worn by players, consisting at the minimum of a shirt, shorts, socks, specialized footwear, and (for goalkeepers) specialized gloves.

Loan: when a player temporarily plays for a club other than the one they are currently contracted to. Such a loan may last from a few weeks to one or more seasons.

Marking: defensive strategy that is either executed man-to-man or by zone, where each player is responsible for a specific area on the pitch.

Match: another word for game.

One touch: style of play in which the ball is passed around quickly using just one touch.

One-two: skill move in which Player One passes the ball to Player Two and runs past the opponent, whereupon they immediately receive the ball back from Player Two in one movement. Also known as a *give-and-go*.

Pitch: playing surface for a game of soccer; usually a specially prepared grass field. Referred to in the Laws of the Game as the field of play.

Set piece: dead ball routine that the attacking team has specifically practiced, such as a free kick taken close to the opposing goal, or a corner kick.

Through-ball: pass from the attacking team that goes straight through the opposition's defense to a teammate who runs to the ball.

Touch line: markings along the side of the pitch, indicating the boundaries of the playing area. Throw-ins are taken from behind this line.

Youth system (academy): young players are contracted to the club and trained to a high standard with the hope that some will develop into professional players. Some clubs provide academic as well as soccer education.

The United States is not a traditional soccer nation. There are plenty of reasons why this is true, and an entire book could easily be dedicated to the topic. For the purposes of this book, the reasons are touched on broadly.

First and foremost, American athletes are distracted by, and attracted to, several other American-invented sports. LeBron James, Tom Brady, and Mike Trout do not play soccer. The sporting heroes of America's young athletes make dunks, not free kicks. They hit home runs, not headers. American kids often grow up playing soccer, but after watching their star athletes play more traditionally American sports, they focus on basketball, football, and baseball instead. Kids just do not grow up in an environment where they are immersed in the sport like they do in Europe or South America, where soccer is king.

Perhaps as a product of the dominance of traditional American sports, coaching in American soccer has understandably not been very good. At the youth level, many coaches are dads with great intentions but little knowledge of the game. To be fair, the sport's governing body, US Soccer, has made great efforts to improve the state of coaching in the game in recent years, but it will be a long time before the quality is top level and universal around the country, and even the youngest kids have coaches with experience and training.

One of the major hurdles has been figuring out how to pay for the needed overhaul in coaching and development, and how to make sure America sees the benefits of the investment. Pouring millions into kids who turn out to be excellent players only to see those players go overseas to play in Europe is a difficult proposition to sell. US Soccer is invested in continuing to improve the game at the Major League Soccer (MLS) level as well, however, so that the young players developed in America have a league to play in that is worthy of their skills.

Despite these challenges, American soccer does have a history with proud moments and players who have worn the red, white, and blue uniforms of the United States Men's National Team (USMNT) with pride. At the World Cup, Team USA has been there from the beginning, and hopes to return to the sport's biggest stage soon.

aspirations: strong desires to achieve something high or great

dispatched: to dispose of something (such as a task or opponent) rapidly or efficiently

flounder: to proceed or act clumsily or ineffectually

CHAPTER 1

A HISTORY OF THE US NATIONAL TEAM

The sport known as football around the world is called soccer in the United States (and in a small handful of other countries, such as Australia, Canada, and Ireland). The actual full name of the sport is association football, derived from the Football Association (FA), which was founded in London in 1863. The FA established common rules for the sport, and future matches played using these were said to be played under "association rules." The term "soccer" comes from the third through fifth letters of "association." The name was shortened simply to football in England before it spread to the rest of the world, but in America, soccer eventually became the preferred term for association football.

Versions of the sport existed in America before association rules. It was popular at universities but rules varied from school to school, and the schools did not compete against each other. After 1865, colleges began adopting association rules for the sport, and in 1876 Rutgers and Princeton played the first intercollegiate match in the United States, won 6–4 by Rutgers.

Soccer thrived in the latter part of the nineteenth century as the country swelled with immigrants from the United Kingdom—from the already heavily populated eastern cities through the Midwest and eventually all the way to

These Canadian players, along with those in places like Australia and Ireland, are from one of the few countries to call the sport soccer

The first intercollegiate soccer match in the United States took place at Rutgers University against arch-rival Princeton in 1869

the West Coast. In 1884, the American Football Association (AFA) was founded in Newark, New Jersey, and was the first attempt at establishing a governing body for the sport, although its membership was limited to the surrounding region. The first United States national team played its first international match against Canada in 1885.

Another governing body calling itself the American Amateur Football Association (AAFA) formed in 1911, but this one had national **aspirations**. Several member groups defected from the AFA to the AAFA, and the AAFA rebranded itself as the United States Football Association (USFA) in 1913. That year, it was the USFA that was recognized by soccer's international governing body, the Swiss-based FIFA (Fédération Internationale de Football Association).

In 1916, the first-ever USFA national team traveled to Europe, playing six matches in Sweden and Norway. It won three of the six matches it played, including a 3–2 win over Sweden to open the tour.

The next major international splash for the national team came at the 1924 Olympic Games in Paris. This was the first Olympic tournament for which the United States had qualified a team. With 22 teams, this would be the biggest international soccer tournament until the 1982 World Cup. The 17-member team was led by coach George Burford, and ranged in age from 20 to 33. Ten teams qualified for a first-round bye, but the Americans were not one of these. They played against Estonia in round one, and won 1–0 on a penalty kick from center forward Andy Straden. This set up a match against South American powerhouse Uruguay, which easily beat the USA 3–0 on its way to the gold medal.

At this time, the national team was composed of amateur players who came together for matches only a few times each year. The team again made the Olympics in 1928 in the Netherlands. Burford returned as coach, but this group proved to be less successful for him. The Americans drew a first round matchup against a skillful side from Argentina, and were embarrassed 11–2.

October 29, 1929 was Black Tuesday in the United States. On that day, the US stock market crashed, initiating the Great Depression, which was the longest and deepest economic decline of the twentieth century. Millions of Americans lost their jobs, and the sport of soccer was not immune to the effects of these hardships. The American Soccer League, a professional league that had existed since 1921, struggled as people could no longer afford to pay to watch soccer. The league would eventually fold in 1932.

The United States Football Association was recognized by FIFA in 1913

At the first-ever World Cup in Uruguay in 1930, the US Men's National Team lost its semifinal match 6–1 to Argentina at Estadio Centenario in Montevideo

On the international stage, however, the US game continued. As a FIFA affiliate, the United States was invited to participate in the first-ever FIFA World Cup, held in Uruguay in 1930. The USA was one of 13 teams to accept, and it played surprisingly well, winning both group stage matches to win Group 4 and advance to the semifinals. Once again, the obstacle was Argentina, who **dispatched** the USA in definitive fashion, 6–1. The USA did finish third, however.

Soccer was not contested at the 1932 Olympics in Los Angeles due to a dispute between FIFA and the International Olympic Committee (IOC) over amateur rules in the sport, so the next major competition was the 1934 World Cup in Italy. Despite widespread economic hardship at the time, there were 32 countries that applied to participate, so the USA had to win a one match qualifier to be included. After qualifying, the Americans had an unlucky draw, pulling the host Italians in the first round, in which they were soundly beaten 7–1 and eliminated.

As the Great Depression dragged on, soccer fell into obscurity in America and it would be decades before the sport recovered. The USA would manage to qualify for just one of the next 10 World Cups. The national program was more successful at the Olympic level, however, qualifying for the next four Olympic Games.

In 1945, the USFA changed its name to include the term "soccer" for the first time, becoming the United States Soccer Football Association (USSFA). The first major tournament for the USSFA was the 1948 Olympic Games in London. The Americans were ousted quickly from the Olympic tournament, losing badly to Italy 9–0.

After the Great Depression, soccer fell into obscurity in America

The North American Soccer League started play in 1968. Soccer legend Pelé played his last-ever match for the New York Cosmos before the league folded in 1984

In 1950, the USA qualified for what would be its last World Cup for 40 years. The tournament was held in Brazil, and despite a win over England, the USA was eliminated in the group stage.

The year 1950 also saw the establishment of the National Soccer Hall of Fame by the Philadelphia Old-Timers Association. They announced 15 initial inductees, including national team standouts Billy Gonsalves, the "Babe Ruth of American soccer," and Charles Spalding, who scored America's first-ever international goal against Sweden in 1916. A physical building for the hall did not come until 1979 in Oneonta, New York. The Hall of Fame was officially recognized in 1983.

1. USA vs. Mexico – 2002 World Cup

The heavily favored Mexicans were the seventh-ranked team in the world by FIFA and came into this round of 16 match undefeated in the tournament after winning Group G. The USA qualified as the second team out of Group D, having given up more goals than they scored. The 2–0 USA win, led by goals from Brian McBride and Landon Donovan, and great play from keeper Brad Friedel, put the USMNT into the quarterfinals, the team's best result since 1930.

2. USA vs. Spain – 2009 Confederations Cup

The USMNT was not supposed to have a chance in the semifinal matchup of this tournament that pits the champions of the world's soccer confederations against each other. Spain was the champion of Europe and had not lost a match in almost three years. The USA were unimpressed, attacking and being rewarded by a Jozy Altidore first-half goal. The American defense was outstanding, and a late goal by Clint Dempsey completed the "Miracle on Grass" and a 2–0 win.

3. USA vs. England – 1950 World Cup

Many believe the result of this match to be the biggest upset in World Cup history. The English side was one of the favorites to win the tournament. The USMNT was made up of part-time players, and everyone expected them to be slaughtered in this match. England controlled the play from beginning to end but could not score against Frank Borghi, a hearse driver from Saint Louis. When Joe Gaetjens scored off a diving header late in the first half, it was all the underdogs would need.

4. USA vs. Trinidad and Tobago – 1989 World Cup Qualifying

The United States really needed this one. Earlier in 1989, FIFA had awarded the United States the 1994 World Cup but the USMNT had not qualified for a tournament since 1950. There was a lot of grumbling about America's selection as hosts when the USMNT had been so bad for so long. That changed in Trinidad and Tobago the day that the USMNT won 1–0 to earn a spot in the 1990 World Cup. The team has qualified for every World Cup since.

5. USA vs. Algeria – 2010 World Cup

This group stage match is certainly not the most important or impactful in USMNT history, but it may be the most exciting. The USA needed a win to advance to the next round; anything less meant elimination. Things looked bleak for the USA as the match ticked into the final minute tied 0–0. That is when an attack orchestrated by Altidore and Dempsey was finished off by Donovan to secure the 1–0 win in the dying seconds of the match.

In 1952, the American team faced the Italians in the first round of the Helsinki Olympics soccer tournament, and were again beaten badly, 8–0. In 1956, the USA received a first round bye at the Melbourne Olympics as just 11 teams competed. That only delayed the usual humiliation, as the Americans were thumped 9–1 by Hungary in the next round.

In the 1960s, the US national program truly began to **flounder**. The team did not qualify for a World Cup or an Olympic Games. Soccer struggled to be relevant at a professional level on the national sports scene. In 1968, the North American Soccer League (NASL) was formed. The league had some success from attracting aging international superstars at the end of their careers, but those successes were short-lived. By 1983, both the NASL and the national team were in trouble. The league was on the verge of failure and Team USA was almost non existent, having played just two matches between 1981 and 1983. The United States Soccer Federation (USSF) (the USSFA changed its name in 1974) made a desperate attempt to raise the profile of the national team by entering it in the NASL for the 1983 season. This experiment was a dismal failure and ended after the so-called Team America finished in last place. The NASL folded the next year.

The 1984 Olympics were held in Los Angeles and Team USA automatically qualified as one of the 16 teams. In a show of patriotism, 78,000 fans turned up at Stanford Stadium to watch the opening match for Team USA against Costa Rica. The young Americans won handily 3–0. Although the team failed to win either of its two remaining matches and was eliminated, the result was at least encouraging, as was a 1–1 draw against Argentina at the 1988 Olympics in South Korea.

The United States had mounted a bid to host the 1994 World Cup and its selection as host in 1989 was heavily criticized due to the perceived weakness of the national program and lack of a professional league. Later that year, however, Team USA built on its Olympic results by qualifying for the 1990 World Cup in Italy. Despite not winning a match at that tournament, the effort legitimized America as a host nation.

The USA qualified for the 1990 World Cup but failed to win a match at the tournament

As host in 1994, Team USA qualified automatically, and drew into Group A with Romania, Switzerland, and Colombia. The Americans tied the Swiss 1–1 and Colombia shockingly lost 3–1 to Romania to open Group A play, meaning the Colombians were desperate for a win against the USA when they met in the second match. The score was 0-0 in the latter stages of the second half when disaster struck for Colombia. Defender Andrés Escobar, the Colombian captain, was sprinting back toward his goal in the middle of the field during an attack by the USA. American John Harkes crossed the ball into the middle, and Escobar slid and stuck out his leg to try to block the cross. Instead, he deflected the ball directly past his helpless keeper into his own goal. Colombia could not recover, giving up a second goal in the second half and losing 2–1. The USA advanced and Colombia was eliminated.

00:00

Check out the highlights from the USMNT win over Colombia at the 1994 World Cup

The win was huge for US Soccer (as the USSF is commonly known). It did not matter that eventual champions Brazil eliminated the USA in the next round. The whole country had been watching and the sport made the most of the attention. Major League Soccer, the still-thriving professional outdoor league, began play in 1996 as part of the legacy of the 1994 World Cup. Team USA again qualified for the World Cup in 1998. The USMNT qualified for eight tournaments in a row before shockingly missing the cut in 2018 after a disappointing qualifying effort. After 40 years in the darkness of World Cup exclusion, Team USA spent the next 28 years in the light of World Cup inclusion. Now Team USA will look to start a new streak in 2022.

TEXT-DEPENDENT QUESTIONS:

1. What is the actual full name of the sport Americans call soccer?

2. Name two of the inaugural inductees to the National Soccer Hall of Fame.

3. In what year did the United States host the World Cup?

RESEARCH PROJECT:

Put together a report on the 1924 Olympic soccer team. Identify each of the 17 players by name and position, and then provide a short history of their background and soccer career, including what they went on to do after the Olympics.

WORDS TO UNDERSTAND:

dispute: a disagreement or argument

redemption: the act of making up for a fault or mistake

sanctions: actions taken by one or more states toward another state as a penalty, or which are calculated to force it to comply with legal obligations

CHAPTER 2

TEAM USA AT THE WORLD CUP

The World Cup, the greatest soccer tournament in the world, exists today because of a **dispute** dating back to 1928. At that time, FIFA was running the Olympic soccer tournament, and the most recent games in Amsterdam had just concluded in June. Around this point, FIFA was informed that the organizers of the 1932 Olympics (scheduled to be held in Los Angeles) were dropping soccer from the Games because the sport was unpopular in the United States and they feared low attendance. This, coupled with an ongoing disagreement over the status of amateur players between FIFA and the IOC, prompted FIFA president Jules Rimet to initiate a new world-class tournament.

1930 World Cup

That tournament was the very first World Cup, held in Uruguay in 1930. It was the only World Cup that did not require qualification, and as a member nation of FIFA since 1913, the United States was one of the countries invited to participate. The US team sailed for 18 days on an ocean liner to Montevideo, and it would have been an even longer trip

The 1930 USMNT traveled 18 days on an ocean liner like this one to get to Uruguay for the first-ever World Cup

for European teams. Ultimately, Rimet had to personally convince four teams from Europe to make the journey and compete with seven other teams from the Americas.

The USA drew into Group Four with Paraguay and Belgium, with the format dictating that the four group winners would advance to the semifinals from the round-robin group stage. The Americans opened against Belgium in the later of the opening day matches. The USA won on the strength of goals from Bart McGhee, captain Tom Florie, and Bert Patenaude. Goalkeeper Jimmy Douglas kept a clean sheet in the 3–0 win, and he and Patenaude were the story for the Americans four days later against Paraguay. Patenaude scored twice in the first 15 minutes. His second goal was originally called an own goal as it deflected off Paraguay's Ramon Gonzales. In November of 2006, however, FIFA officially accepted that there was enough evidence to credit Patenaude with the goal. Since he also added a second half goal in the match, he had scored what turned out to be the first hat trick in World Cup history.

The consecutive 3–0 wins put the USA in the semifinals against mighty Argentina, which is where the great effort of the US team ended. Argentina dismantled the Americans 6–1 to eliminate them. The score was just 1–0 at halftime but defender Ralph Tracey could not play the second half due to a broken leg, and no substitutions were allowed in those days. Therefore the USA played with 10 men, including Douglas, who had badly sprained his ankle in the first half. Given this, the match quickly became lopsided in the second half.

The Americans did come away with third place in the tournament, which they won by forfeit as Yugoslavia refused to play the third place match. This first-ever result for the United States is still the best ever in a World Cup for the men's team.

1934 World Cup

Four years later, the tournament was hosted by Italy, mostly to appease FIFA's European members. This, of course, upset the South American countries and many of them, including defending champions Uruguay, refused to take part. The United States was a late entry and ended up playing its qualifying match against Mexico in Italy three days before the start of the tournament. Both teams traveled to Europe knowing that only

Italy celebrates its victory at the 1934 World Cup.
Italy beat the United States 7–1 to open the tournament

one would compete in the World Cup. The USA won 4–2. The reward was an opening match in what was now a single elimination tournament against host Italy. The Italians embarrassed them 7–1.

1950 World Cup

The United States failed to qualify for the 1938 World Cup. Following that, war caused the cancellation of the event until 1950, when the tournament was held in Brazil. Germany and Japan were banned due to post-war **sanctions**. Mostly for political reasons, several Eastern European countries refused to participate, including Czechoslovakia and Hungary. Other countries cited travel costs and logistics as the reason for skipping the tournament. Ultimately, only 13 teams competed in the two-stage round-robin tournament, including the United States.

The American team lost two of its three opening stage matches and did not advance. The match it did win, however, is one of the most famous victories in World Cup history. The English team came to Brazil as a legitimate threat to win the tournament and won its opening match against Chile 2–0. The USA lost its opener to Spain, and the

England's superstar player Stanley Matthews (seen here being mobbed by autograph seekers in Holland in 1957) was available to play against the USA in the 1950 World Cup match, but was rested so he could be fresh for supposedly tougher opponents later on. England lost 1–0

stage seemed set for an easy English win when their team played the Americans in the next match. American coach Bill Jefferey openly declared that his team had no chance to win but US goalkeeper Frank Borghi refused to believe it. He made two brilliant saves in the first 12 minutes to open the match. He made another stop on a header in the 32nd minute. Then the improbable happened just 5 minutes later. Joe Gaetjens got his head on a shot by teammate Walter Bahr to guide the ball past English goalkeeper Bert Williams and into the goal. In the second half, the English attacked relentlessly but two more spectacular saves by Borghi kept them off the scoresheet. The shocking 1–0 loss, combined with another 1–0 loss to Spain, eliminated England.

1990 World Cup

The win in 1950 was the last success for the United States at the World Cup for a long time. The USA failed to qualify for the next nine tournaments—a span of 40 years. By 1990, however, there had been some encouraging signs for the US national program: the team had just missed qualifying for the 1986 World Cup and had qualified for the 1988 Olympics. During qualification for the 1990 World Cup in Italy, FIFA announced that the United States would be the host nation for the 1994 event. The move drew heavy criticism from other FIFA members as the US team was perceived to be weak and the sport was not popular in America. After all, the United States had not qualified for 40 years and had no professional outdoor league. That perception changed in 1989,, however, when the USA qualified for the 1990 World Cup by beating Trinidad and Tobago. The Americans did not win a match in that World Cup, but it laid a foundation for being the hosts in 1994.

The USA qualified for the 1990 World Cup with a crucial win over Trinidad and Tobago. It was the first World Cup qualification for the USA in 40 years

1994 World Cup

The US team made a good showing in the 1994 tournament. Drawing into a group with Switzerland, Colombia, and Romania, it opened play against the Swiss and managed a 1–1 draw. In its second match against the heavily favored Colombians, the scoring opened when Colombian defender Andrés Escobar redirected a cross from American John Harkes into his own goal. Colombia could not recover from this huge mistake and the Americans won 2–1. Upon returning home to Colombia after the team's elimination, Escobar received dozens of death threats and, tragically, was soon murdered in retaliation for that own goal against the USA. The Americans, on the other hand, advanced to the second round against Brazil, but lost 1–0.

2002 World Cup

A horrible effort at the 1998 World Cup in France saw the United States finish dead last out of 32 teams after managing just a single goal in group play. The team managed to qualify for the 2002 World Cup in South Korea and Japan, where it was looking for redemption. It drew into Group D with Portugal, South Korea, and Poland. The USA opened against Portugal and surprised the Portuguese by jumping out to a 3–0 first half lead, aided by a Portuguese own goal. The Americans

 SIDEBAR: WORLD CUP LEADERS

These are the men who have been captain for the USMNT during a World Cup tournament.

PLAYER	WORLD CUP	CAPS AS CAPTAIN	TOTAL CAPS
Tom Florie	1930	4	8
George Moorehouse	1934	1	7
Ed McIlvenny	1950	1	3
Harry Keough	1950	6	19
Walter Bahr	1950	11	19
Michael Windischmann	1990	39	50
Tony Meola	1994	15	100
Thomas Dooley	1998	10	81
Earnie Stewart	2002	9	101
Claudio Reyna	2002, 2006	46	112
Carlos Bocanegra	2010	63	110
Clint Dempsey	2014	21	134

held on in the second half to win 3–2. Next up for the Americans was host South Korea, who was playing in front of more than 60,000 fans at Daegu Stadium. Again, the USA had a strong start, with a first half goal from Clint Mathis. But the South Koreans pressed throughout the match. Strong play from Man of the Match keeper Brad Friedel kept the Americans ahead until the equalizer finally came in the 78th minute. The 1–1 draw was enough for the USA to advance to the knockout stage.

In the round of 16, the United States faced familiar CONCACAF foe Mexico. American stars Brian McBride and Landon Donovan provided first and second half goals, respectively, to go along with a clean sheet from Friedel. The USA won 2–0 to advance to the quarterfinals, the best American showing since 1930.

Watch highlights from the 2002 World Cup quarterfinals against Germany

The quarterfinal opponent was mighty Germany, the three-time World Cup champions. German goalkeeper and captain Oliver Kahn made two great saves against Donovan in the first half before Michael Ballack was able to beat Friedel on a header off a free kick from the right side of the box. The Americans pressed in the second half, led by captain Claudio Reyna. They were unlucky off of a corner kick when a German hand ball on the goal line went unnoticed by the referees and Germany held on for the 1–0 win.

2006–14 World Cups

Since that 2002 quarterfinal appearance, the United States has enjoyed moderate success in the World Cups that have followed. 2006 was not a good year as the Americans failed to win a match and were eliminated following the group stage in Germany.

In 2010 in South Africa, however, the United States went undefeated in the group stage with a win and two draws. These results allowed the Americans to win their group and advance to face Ghana in round two. In that match, Donovan scored his third goal of the tournament, but Ghana won 2–1, and the USA was eliminated in 12th place.

In 2014 in Brazil, the USA drew into a difficult group with Germany, Portugal and Ghana. The United States opened against Ghana and avenged the 2010 defeat by winning 2–1. Match two came against Portugal and superstar Cristiano Ronaldo. Led by captain Clint Dempsey and Man of the Match goalkeeper Tim Howard, the USA managed a 2–2 draw. The final group stage match resulted in a 1–0 loss to Germany, but the USA was able to advance on goal

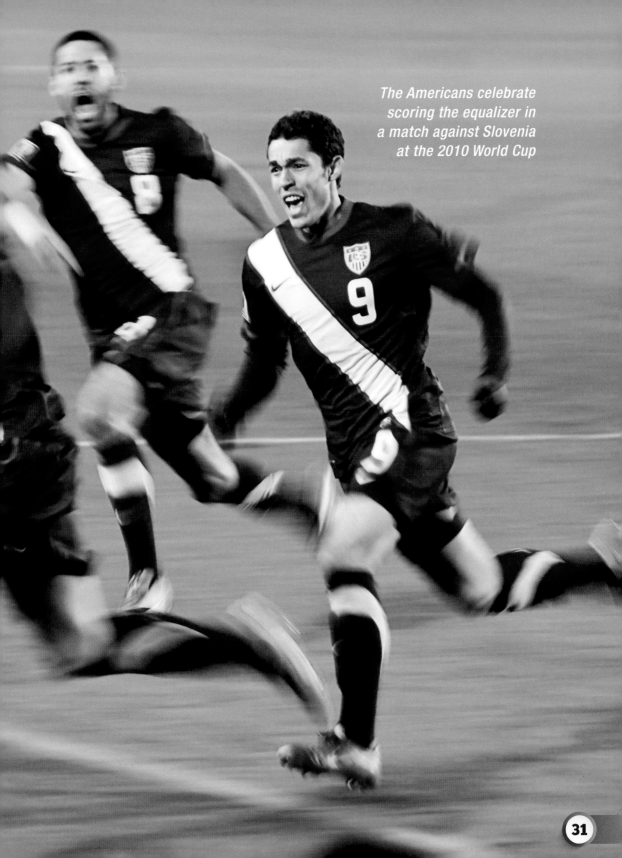

The Americans celebrate scoring the equalizer in a match against Slovenia at the 2010 World Cup

differential over Portugal. In the knockout stage, the Americans faced Belgium, and the tightly played match resulted in no goals being scored in regulation time. Belgium scored twice in extra time to eliminate the USA 2–1.

Team USA had the chance to qualify for the World Cup in Russia in 2018. It came down to the final qualifying match in October 2017 against Trinidad and Tobago, the last place team in the final qualifying group. The Americans needed a draw or better to advance, but lost 2–1 to miss the tournament for the first time since 1986.

A major overhaul is expected to put the team in a position to succeed again by 2022.

The USA and Ghana met in back-to-back World Cups in 2010 and 2014. In 2014, the USA avenged a 2–1 round of 16 loss in 2010 by winning a group stage match with the same score

1. Who was president of FIFA in 1928?
2. Who scored the only goal in the USA's upset of England at the 1950 World Cup?
3. Which American player was named Man of the Match against Portugal in the 2014 World Cup?

 RESEARCH PROJECT:

The USMNT has advanced to the quarterfinals or better only twice in 10 World Cups: in 1930 and 2002. Which of these accomplishments do you think is more impressive? Write a report comparing and contrasting the two results. Be sure to consider tournament format and the quality and depth of competition among the factors you examine in reaching your conclusions.

WORDS TO UNDERSTAND:

hailed: publicly acknowledged for excellence; acclaimed

inaugural: marking the beginning of a new venture, series, etc.

wily: crafty; cunning

CHAPTER 3

PAST STARS OF TEAM USA

Soccer is the ultimate team sport, but the best teams are often successful because great players lead them. In the more than 80-year history of the United States national soccer team, there have been several players who have stepped forward to lead their countrymen on soccer's biggest stage.

Landon Donovan

Landon Donovan is widely considered to be the best player in the history of the USMNT. He grew up in Southern California and started playing soccer at age 6. During high school he was invited to train with the under-17 US Soccer youth development program national team. As a 17-year old, he signed a six-year deal with Bundesliga club Bayer Leverkusen in Germany. Donovan never had much success in Europe, however, and played most of his club career in the United States with MLS, but he thrived on the international stage.

Landon Donovan is the second-leading goal scorer in USMNT history

Check out this career retrospective of Landon Donovan

20th CENTURY TALENT BASE

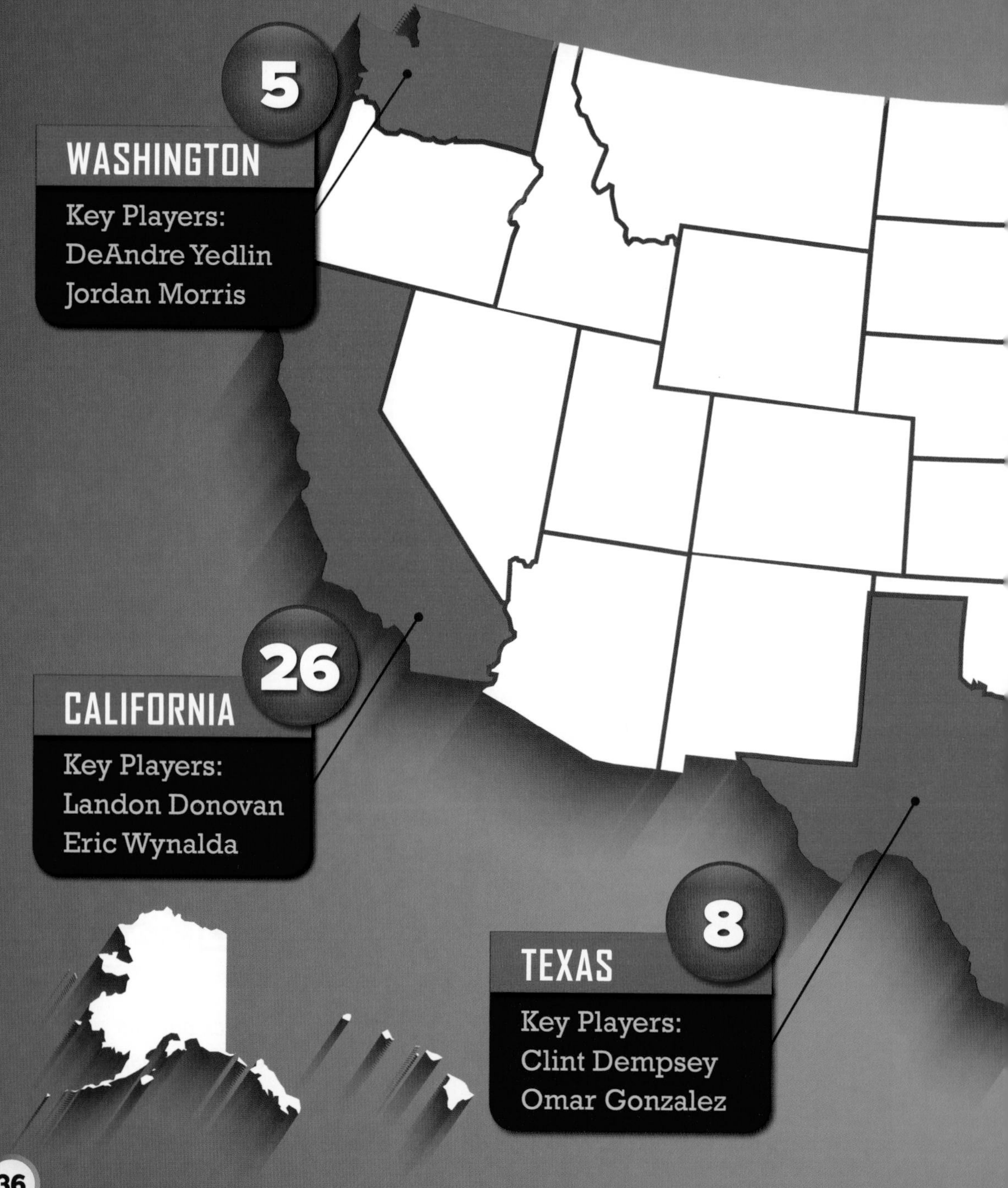

5

WASHINGTON

Key Players:
DeAndre Yedlin
Jordan Morris

26

CALIFORNIA

Key Players:
Landon Donovan
Eric Wynalda

8

TEXAS

Key Players:
Clint Dempsey
Omar Gonzalez

These are the states that have produced the most Team USA members who have played at least five matches since 2000.

NEW JERSEY 10
Key Players:
Tim Howard
Michael Bradley

METRO WASHINGTON DC 8
Key Players:
Oguchi Onyewu
Kyle Beckerman

GEORGIA 5
Key Players:
Clint Mathis
Ricardo Clark

MISSOURI 7
Key Players:
Steve Ralston
Tim Ream

KEY FACTS:
- 143 players have played five or more matches for the USMNT since 2000
- 16 grew up outside the U.S.A
- 127 are U.S. raised and trained
- 65, or more than half, come from just seven areas

SIDEBAR: CAP LEADERS

Here are the players who have made the most appearances for Team USA in their careers as of December 31, 2017.

	PLAYER	CAPS	GOALS	ERA
1	Cobi Jones	164	15	1992–2004
2	Landon Donovan	157	57	2000–14
3	Clint Dempsey*	141	57	2004–
4	Michael Bradley*	140	17	2006–
5	Jeff Agoos	134	4	1988–2003
6	Marcelo Balboa	127	13	1988–2000
7	DaMarcus Beasley*	126	17	2001–
8	Tim Howard*	121	0	2002–
9	Claudio Reyna	112	8	1994–2006
10	Carlos Bocanegra	110	14	2001–12
10	Paul Caligiuri	110	5	1984–97
10	Jozy Altidore*	110	41	2007–

- active

Donovan, who played as a forward or winger, is the all-time leader in assists for his country with 58, and second in all time goals with 57. Of his 57 goals, 5 were scored at the World Cup. At the 2002 World Cup in South Korea and Japan, he helped the United States reach the quarterfinals, and at 20-years old he was named Best Young Player at that tournament. Donovan was named USMNT Player of the Year a record seven times. He retired in 2016.

Claudio Reyna

The sport of soccer was in Claudio Reyna's blood when he was born in New Jersey in 1973. His father was an immigrant from Argentina, where he had a brief professional career. Claudio grew up playing the game, achieving recognition as a two-time national High School Player of the Year. Reyna received a full scholarship to play midfield at the University of Virginia, where he led the Cavaliers to three straight National Collegiate Athletic Association (NCAA) men's soccer national championships. He was a two-time College Player of the Year.

After college, Reyna was named to the 1994 USMNT and made the squad for the World Cup as the United States hosted the tournament. Reyna unfortunately suffered an injury and did not play in the World Cup.
Injuries were an issue that would bother Reyna throughout his career. After the World Cup, he signed to play in Germany with Bayer Leverkusen, and had a 13-year long club career in Europe, setting multiple records for transfer fees for an American player.

Claudio Reyna warms up during a 2006 USMNT training session

Internationally, Reyna played in two Olympics (1992 and 1996) and three World Cups (1998, 2002, and 2006) for the USMNT. He was the team captain in 2002 when the USA made a run to the World Cup quarterfinals. Reyna was named Man of the Match in the quarterfinal against Germany, despite the USA losing 1–0. Not known as a goal scorer, Reyna was **hailed** for his skill at controlling matches from his center midfield position. He is the first and only US player to be named to a FIFA World Cup All-Star Team (2002). Reyna served as US captain for eight years, and was elected to the National Soccer Hall of Fame in 2012.

Brad Friedel

Ohio native Brad Friedel grew up as a multi-sport athlete. The 6'3"
Friedel was an all-state basketball player in Ohio in the 1980s. Later, he
chose to pursue soccer instead, attending UCLA and leading the Bruins
to the NCAA title as a freshman goalkeeper in 1990. Friedel was a two-
time All-American and a College Player of the Year winner in his time at
UCLA.

Friedel played the majority of his club career in the English Premier
League—most successfully with Blackburn. Friedel holds the Premier
League record for most consecutive appearances with 310.

Internationally, he played 82 games as keeper for the USMNT, beginning
in 1992. He was the backup keeper at both the 1994 and 1998 World
Cups. He started the final group stage match in 1998 after Kasey Keller
struggled in allowing four goals in the first two group stage losses.
Friedel and the USA lost 1–0 to Yugoslavia in his World Cup debut.
By the 2002 World Cup, Friedel was the starter, and helped his team
advance past the group stage, then kept a clean sheet against Mexico
in the round of 16. The best U.S. showing since 1930 ended with a 1–0
loss to Germany in the following round. Friedel retired in 2015 and was
named head coach of the U.S. men's under-19 team in 2016.

Brian McBride

Striker Brian McBride grew up in the suburbs of Chicago in the 1970s
and '80s. As a high school junior, he led his team to the Illinois state
championship. He played college soccer at the University of Saint Louis,
where he scored 72 goals in 89 career games and was an All-American
in 1993.

McBride was the number one pick in the first-ever MLS draft, and played
most of his club career at home in the MLS, except for a successful stint
with Fulham in England's Premier League. After his first three and a half
years with the club, McBride was named Fulham team captain, and was
back-to-back Club Player of the year in 2007 and 2008.

For Team USA, McBride played 95 matches in his career, including
appearances at three World Cup tournaments (1998, 2002, and 2006).

He scored three World Cup goals in his career, including the winning goals against both Portugal and Mexico at the 2002 tournament. McBride is one of only five players with at least 30 international goals for Team USA. He retired in 2010, and was elected to the National Soccer Hall of Fame in 2015.

Eric Wynalda

Eric Wynalda was always good at scoring goals. The **wily** striker started scoring young as a kid in Southern California, where one season he outscored his entire youth soccer division by himself. Wynalda went on to star at San Diego State University before leaving to join the USMNT for the 1990 World Cup in Italy, where he played in two matches.

Chicago native Brian McBride played at the University of Saint Louis before joining the USMNT in 1993

By 1994, Wynalda was an established star, playing professionally in the German Bundesliga and scoring 14 goals for the USMNT. He scored the first goal for the United States as the host nation opened the 1994 World Cup against Switzerland in front of 73,000 fans near Detroit. The USA was eliminated against Brazil in the round of 16. Four years later, Wynalda played in two of the three matches in a disappointing USA showing in France in 1998, where the team scored just a single goal.

After retiring from the USMNT in 2000, Eric Wynalda began working as a soccer analyst on televised matches

Eddie Pope (#23) battles Landon Donovan (#10) for the ball at the 2004 MLS All-Star game. Pope and Donovan were teammates on two World Cup squads for the USMNT

Wynalda continued to excel away from the World Cup stage, scoring 19 more international goals in World Cup qualifiers and CONCACAF Gold Cup tournaments. His 34 goals was the all-time record for Team USA when Wynalda retired from the USMNT in 2000. He was named US Player of the Decade for the 1990s, and elected to the National Soccer Hall of Fame in 2004.

Tab Ramos

Tab Ramos is not American by birth. Ramos moved with his family from Uruguay to New Jersey in 1977, when Ramos was 11. He became a US citizen while in high school in 1982. As a high school player, Ramos was a two-time All-American at midfield and the 1983 National High School Player of the Year. Ramos went on to play all four years at North Carolina State University, where he was a three-time All-American midfielder.

Ramos played most of his professional club career in the Spanish second division. He was the first player to sign in the newly formed MLS, where he finished his career.

Ramos first played with the US national program at the under-20 level in 1982, and joined the USMNT in 1988. He was Wynalda's teammate at the 1990, 1994, and 1998 World Cups. Ramos played 81 matches for his country, a number limited by injury over the course of his career. Known more for his superb defensive skills, Ramos's best-known offensive highlight came in qualifying for the 1998 World Cup. In Portland during a must-win match for the USA against Costa Rica, Ramos scored by burying a lovely assist from Marcelo Balboa from the top of the box in front of a sold-out crowd.

After retiring in 2002, Ramos was elected to the National Soccer Hall of Fame in 2005. He began coaching the under-20 US men's team in 2011.

Eddie Pope

Eddie Pope was a defender who grew up playing the game near Greensboro, North Carolina. After high school, he was recruited to play for the nearby University of North Carolina, where he earned All-American honors in 1994.

Pope was the second overall pick in the 1996 MLS draft and played his entire club career in the domestic league. His career with the USMNT began that same year. During his tenure, he was the unquestioned first-team player at his position. Pope's strength as a center back came in winning battles for balls in the air. He was strong, fast, and big, and was a steadying presence on the back line through three World Cups (1998, 2002, and 2006).

Pope played a total of 82 matches—all starts—for Team USA. His eight total goals were the least of his contributions. After retiring in 2007, Pope was elected to the National Soccer Hall of Fame in 2011.

Adelino "Billy" Gonsalves

American soccer came of age around the turn of this century, a time that saw some of the country's best international results and produced some of its greatest players. America's first superstar, however, had his heyday about 80 years ago. Adelino "Billy" Gonsalves was known as the "Babe Ruth of American Soccer" in his time. His parents immigrated to New England from Portugal two years before his birth in 1908.

At 19, Gonsalves had made a name for himself as an attacking midfielder in local leagues, attracting the attention of the American Soccer League Club in Boston. He signed with the pro team and scored 52 goals in two seasons before going home to Fall River, Massachusetts, to play with the Marksmen there. He led Fall River to back-to-back National Challenge Cup titles, the sport's national championship.

This success put Gonsalves on the national program radar and he was selected to play for the United States in the 1930 World Cup in Uruguay, and again in 1934 in Italy. Gonsalves was a member of the **inaugural** class of the National Soccer Hall of Fame in 1950.

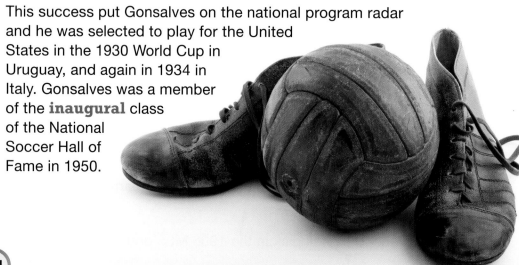

TEXT-DEPENDENT QUESTIONS:

1. Where did Landon Donovan grow up?
2. Where did Eric Wynalda play college soccer?
3. When was Billy Gonsalves inducted into the National Soccer Hall of Fame?

RESEARCH PROJECT:

American soccer has had several great players who could also have been mentioned in this chapter. Choose two more American players who had great international careers for the USMNT and create a chart that compares and contrasts the players, outlining what made them great.

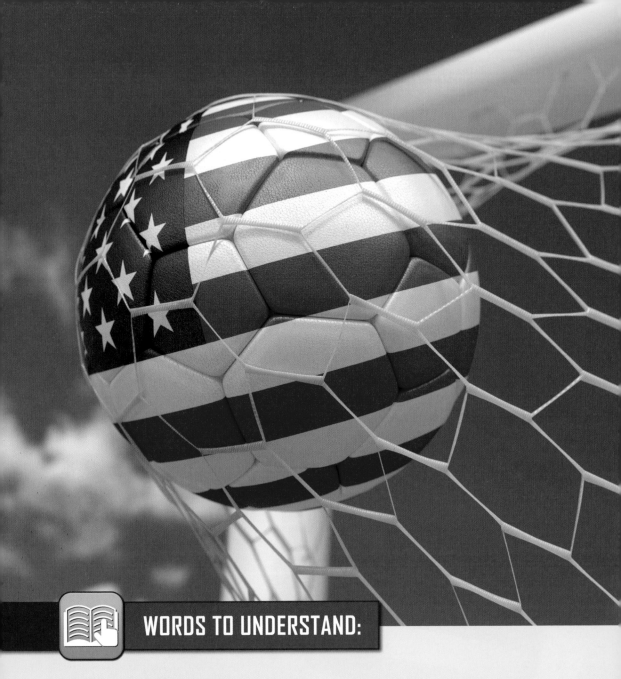

WORDS TO UNDERSTAND:

legacies: things handed down by a predecessor

phenom: derived from the word phenomenon, this describes a person who is outstandingly talented or admired, especially an up-and-comer

torrid: scorching hot

CHAPTER 4

TODAY'S STARS OF TEAM USA

The colossal failure to qualify for the 2018 World Cup may tarnish the **legacies** of some of the Team USA veterans. The young stars of the squad will likely have a shot at redemption with an opportunity to qualify for Qatar in 2022, but for those already in their thirties, competing in 2022 is a long shot. It would be a shame if this is the case, as many of today's veteran players are among the best to ever wear the red, white and blue. Only time will tell how history will remember their efforts for Team USA.

Clint Dempsey

The veteran former captain of the US side, Clint Dempsey is America's all-time leading goal scorer, and still has deadly striking ability more than 140 appearances into his USMNT career.

Born in 1983, Dempsey came out of rural east Texas in the late 1990s to play with the Dallas Texans, a well regarded youth soccer club

Clint Dempsey got his professional start with MLS when the New England Revolution drafted him out of Furman University

Midfielder Michael Bradley is the current captain of the USMNT

in Texas. Dempsey's family had limited means, so the six-hour round trip to Dallas so he could play was a significant sacrifice. Dempsey made it all worthwhile when he received a scholarship to play at Furman University. Dempsey played well enough to be the eighth pick of the 2004 MLS draft. He played his first three club seasons at New England before a record $4 million transfer sent him to the English Premier League to play at Fulham with Brian McBride. There, he became the first American to ever score 50 goals in the Premier League, and he played for seven seasons before returning to MLS.

For the USMNT, Dempsey debuted in 2004 in a qualifier for the 2006 World Cup. He scored his first World Cup goal in that tournament in a loss to Ghana. He scored what was likely his final World Cup goal against Portugal in 2014. The three-time USA Player of the Year will be 39 in 2022.

Michael Bradley steals and stuns with a brilliant goal against Mexico

00:00

DONOVAN AND DEMPSEY:

USMNT CAREER STATS

Caps

Goals

Goals per Match

Assists

World Cup Goals

US Player of the Year

LANDON DONOVAN:

- All-Time Leading Scorer in Major League Soccer - 144 Goals & 136 Assists
- Played in a Record 14 Straight MLS All-Star Games
- Named Best Young Player at the 2002 World Cup

TWO USA GREATS
PAST AND PRESENT

DONOVAN	DEMPSEY
157	141
57	57
.36	.40
58	21
5	4
4	3

As of Sep 15, 2017

CLINT DEMPSEY:

- Member of Three USA World Cup Teams
- Team USA Captain at the 2014 World Cup
- Scored 57 Goals in the English Premier League - most by an American Player

Michael Bradley

Michael Bradley has known little else but soccer for his entire life. The USMNT midfielder is the son of Bob Bradley, the longtime college, professional, and former national team coach. Bradley had, in fact, just debuted for the national team when his father was hired as manager following the 2006 World Cup. At the time, Bradley was already in his third MLS season at age 19, having entered the league right out of high school.

Bradley was not chosen for the 2006 World Cup team but soon became a starter in midfield with his father as coach. Over the years, he has flourished as a player and a leader. Bradley was instrumental in leading the USA to a Confederations Cup final appearance in 2009. He was named USMNT captain in 2015 by his father's successor, Jürgen Klinsmann, who took over in 2011. Bradley remained the starting center half for Klinsmann in every US game at each of the 2010 and 2014 World Cups.

Christian Pulisic

Christian Pulisic is the youngest player on Team USA and is poised to become the face of the sport in America for the next 15 years. He was born in 1998 in Hershey, Pennsylvania. Like his midfield partner Bradley, Pulisic grew up around the sport because his father was a soccer coach. A **phenom** at the sport, Pulisic quickly drew attention from Europe, where he visited Barcelona, Chelsea, Porto, and others before he signed to play with the youth academy of German Bundesliga side Borussia Dortmund at age 16. After scoring 10 times in only 15 games, Pulisic was promoted to the senior side.

This success in Europe did not go unnoticed by Klinsmann. Pulisic had scored 49 goals in 62 appearances for the under-15 and under-17 U.S. national teams, and so just two months after his Bundesliga debut, Klinsmann put Pulisic on the USMNT for a World Cup qualifying match against Guatemala. Two months later, Pulisic became the youngest American player to score a goal for the USMNT. He scores at a **torrid** pace with nine goals in his first 20 Team USA matches.

Tim Howard

Tim Howard is a big man. His 6'3", 210 lb. frame is one of his advantages as a world-class soccer goalkeeper. The New Jersey native also possesses uncanny reflexes, which has led to dozens of exciting, acrobatic saves in his more than 100 matches in goal for the USMNT.

As late as high school, Howard played midfield, but soon transitioned to goalkeeper full time. By age 16 he was on the radar of the national program, and three years later he played for both the under-20 and under-23 teams in international tournaments. Behind the great Brad Friedel on the depth chart, Howard would wait until 2002 to debut for the USNMT.

After the 2006 World Cup, when again, like in 1998, the USA failed to advance past the group stage with Keller in goal, Howard was given the starting job by Bob Bradley, and he has held it ever since. No goalkeeper has more wins or caps for the USMNT than Howard. With him in goal, the USA advanced to the second round in both the 2010 and 2014 World Cups. Howard will be 43 in 2022, so his World Cup career is likely over.

Tim Howard took over as the starting goalkeeper for the USMNT following the 2006 World Cup

Howard began, and now continues, his club career in the MLS, bookending a stellar 13-year stint in the Premier League, primarily with Everton.

John Brooks

Germany is a hotbed of soccer passion and it is one of the most successful World Cup nations of all time. It is little wonder that John Brooks grew up loving the game, since the American was born and raised in Berlin. His father was in the military and stationed in Germany, where Brooks learned to excel at the sport. He played for Bundesliga side Hertha BSC's youth team, eventually debuting for the senior team in 2012 at age 19.

Defender John Brooks will play in his second World Cup for the USMNT in Russia in 2018

The defender made six appearances for the under-20 and under-23 US national teams. His senior team debut came in 2013 against Bosnia and Herzegovina. Brooks played in the USA's opening match of the 2014 World Cup at age 21. It was his only appearance in four US matches, but it was memorable. On as a second half substitute, he scored the winning goal against Ghana with four minutes left to secure the only win of the tournament for the USA.

Jozy Altidore

The other veteran forward for the USMNT, Floridian Jozy Altidore, has appeared in more than 100 matches for the squad since 2007. Altidore has played most of his club career in Europe, mostly with Alkmaar Zaanstreek in the Dutch Eredivisie and Sunderland in the Premier League. Like many of his USMNT teammates, he began as a professional in MLS and returned to the league in 2015.

Altidore played youth soccer at the private IMG Academy boarding school beginning at age 14, where he trained with the under-17 US team. Three years later, he debuted with the senior team. Altidore has represented the United States at both the 2010 and 2014 World Cup tournaments. He played every match in 2010, but his 2014 experience was cut short by an opening match injury. In 2016, Altidore was named US Soccer Male Athlete of the Year.

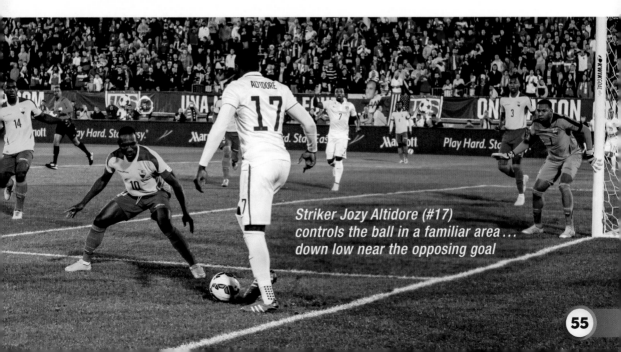

Striker Jozy Altidore (#17) controls the ball in a familiar area... down low near the opposing goal

SIDEBAR: THE NCAA AND THE USMNT

In 1989, all but one of the players on the USMNT was a current or former player from a National Collegiate Athletic Association (NCAA) program. By 2015, that number had dropped to just two. When Clint Dempsey came out of Furman University in 1993, about half of his USMNT teammates were NCAA products. In 2017, only Dempsey, DeAndre Yedlin, and Darlington Nagbe had played college soccer. Most top tier players now come through development academies or turn pro out of high school. The influence of the NCAA on the USMNT may be dwindling, but the NCAA legacy is noteworthy. Here are the schools that have produced the most senior team members:

UCLA – 14

The Bruin program came to prominence under German-born coach Sigi Schmid in the 1980s. Schmid built the program into a powerhouse over 19 seasons, winning three national titles at his alma mater before moving to manage in MLS.

Prominent players: Carlos Bocanegra, 110 USMNT caps, 63 as captain. Brad Friedel, 82 USMNT caps, 4 as captain. Cobi Jones, 164 USMNT caps, 4 as captain. Paul Caligiuri, 110 USMNT caps.

Maryland – 7

Head coach Sasho Cirovski has managed the Terrapins for more than 20 seasons. His best teams were those in the 2000s, which won national titles in 2005 and 2008.

Prominent player: Graham Zusi, 51 USMNT caps.

Virginia – 6

USMNT manager Bruce Arena coached the Cavaliers for 18 seasons in the 1980s and '90s, winning national titles from 1991–94. The program is still among the best, winning titles in 2009 and 2014 under coach George Gelnovatch.

Prominent players: Claudio Reyna, 112 USMNT caps, 46 as captain.

DeAndre Yedlin

Defender DeAndre Yedlin is already a World Cup veteran at age 24 . The Seattle native got in as a substitute in three of the four USA matches in 2014, but is now one of Team USA's starting defenders at right back.

Yedlin left Seattle for college in Akron, Ohio to play for the Zips in 2011. After two years at school, he left for a professional contract with his hometown MLS club, the Sounders. After two seasons in Seattle, he left MLS for the Premier League, and continues to play in England.

Despite his youth, Yedlin already has more than 50 caps for Team USA. Known more in his early career for his superior foot speed than his defending, Yedlin has steadily improved the defensive skills that will make him an essential part of the USMNT in the future.

Defender DeAndre Yedlin (#2) has played nearly 50 matches representing his country

Darlington Nagbe

Darlington Nagbe was just a baby when his mother fled their war-torn homeland of Liberia in 1990 with him and his brother. The family lived in several places in Europe before moving to Cleveland in 2001. Following in the footsteps of his father, a professional soccer player, Nagbe excelled at the beautiful game growing up. He eventually went to the University of Akron to play, leaving the year before Yedlin's arrival. Nagbe and the Zips won the NCAA national championship in 2010 and Nagbe was named College Player of the Year.

At the club level, Nagbe was drafted by Portland of MLS in 2011 and has played his entire pro career there. At the national level, Nagbe is a relative newcomer as he did not become a US citizen until 2015, making him ineligible until then for the USMNT. Nagbe never started for Klinsmann, but Arena has other plans.

Following a World Cup qualifying match in June of 2017 that saw Nagbe in the starting lineup for Arena, the manager said of his midfielder, "I think he's an exceptional player. I think he's a very talented kid. He's just beginning to experience this level . . . I believe in him."

Darling: ates

TEXT-DEPENDENT QUESTIONS:

1. In what year was Clint Dempsey born?
2. Where was USMNT defender John Brooks born and raised?
3. In what year did USMNT midfielder Darlington Nagbe become a US citizen?

RESEARCH PROJECT:

Write an in-depth report on USMNT rising star Christian Pulisic. Detail his background, his rise to prominence in the sport, and address why so many experts predict he will be the best American player of all time.

WORDS TO UNDERSTAND:

coherent: logical and consistent

dire: extremely serious or urgent

domestically: relating to, made in, or done in a person's own country

viable: capable of working, functioning, or developing adequately

CHAPTER 5

THE FUTURE OF TEAM USA

Before looking ahead to where the sport is going **domestically**, there is value in looking back at where it has come from. American soccer has come a long way in the last 30 years. In 1989, the United States won the bid to host the 1994 World Cup. The decision was controversial as the USMNT had failed to qualify for a World Cup tournament since 1950, meaning it had missed nine consecutive events. Even at the Olympic level, the United States had failed to win a match since 1984.

With the announcement of the successful World Cup bid, however, fortunes took a positive turn for the sport in the United States. Four months after the country won the bid on Independence Day 1989, the USMNT beat Trinidad and Tobago 1–0 to qualify for the 1990 World Cup. The fact that the United States had earned its place in the 1990 tournament legitimized winning the 1994 bid in the eyes of many.

Questra
1994

The USMNT did not do particularly well at the 1990 tournament, losing all three of its matches. Qualification, however, was still progress. Perhaps the most progressive outcome of winning the 1994 bid was due to one of the attached conditions that came with acceptance. US Soccer was required to commit to the establishment of a top-level professional outdoor league. Such a league had not existed in the United States since the North American Soccer League folded in 1985.

The United States won the bid for the 1994 World Cup just four months before its team qualified for the 1990 tournament in Italy

In the early days of Major League Soccer, teams played in football stadiums where large sections of the stands were unsold, and matches were poorly attended

In 1993, the intent to organize and form the league was announced, and following the successfully staged 1994 World Cup, Major League Soccer (MLS) was formed in 1995 with the ABC and ESPN TV networks already onboard with broadcast rights contracts. Despite the boost in soccer's profile from the World Cup, however, the new league struggled when it launched with 10 teams in 1996.

Attendance in the first year averaged more than 17,000 fans per game league-wide. In the second year, however, attendance dropped 16 percent. By 2000, it had dropped below 14,000 per game, off almost 21 percent since MLS's debut. League officials scrambled to save the league, scrapping rule changes that had been intended to make the game more appealing to Americans, like a clock that counted down rather than up and a breakaway shootout method to settle ties. The league had already lost $250 million by this point. In November of 2001, MLS nearly folded as the majority of its owners wanted out.

By 2002, the league's 10 teams had a total of only three owners, who had purchased all of the unwanted teams, and player salaries were frozen. The situation was **dire**. And then the 2002 World Cup happened. That year, the USMNT, led by a young Landon Donovan and veterans Claudio Reyna, Brad Friedel, and Brian McBride, captivated the nation by advancing to the quarterfinals and giving Germany all they could handle before losing. Just four months later, more than 60,000 fans attended the MLS Cup championship match between Los Angeles and New England, a more than 280 percent increase over the 2001 crowd, and still the biggest crowd ever for an MLS Cup final.

The largest crowd ever for an MLS Cup final was in New England in 2002

The league adopted a philosophy of trying to recruit and develop homegrown talent, thereby making American players its focus, and fans responded. By 2004, average attendance was up by 13 percent from the low point of 2000. After the 2004 season, MLS announced expansion plans to add one team in Salt Lake City and a second one in Los Angeles. A team was also added in 2007, and again in 2008, but the 2009 launch of a franchise in Seattle was the game changer that showed what soccer in the United States could be.

In Seattle, the Sounders have enjoyed record crowds since entering MLS in 2009

When the Seattle Sounders began play in 2009, the team was an overwhelming success. The expansion team set a MLS record for average attendance. The Sounders broke the record held by the 2008 Los Angeles Galaxy (which had the league high attendance six years running) by 19 percent. Nearly 31,000 people on average attended Sounder games in 2009—and that was the lowest season average the team has ever had. Seattle has broken the record for average attendance in a season five times since then.

Since Seattle's debut, expansion has exploded in MLS. The league grew from 13 teams in 2009 to 23 with the debut of Los Angeles FC in 2018. The designated player rule has allowed teams to make an exception to the salary cap to sign international stars, none bigger than England's David Beckham, who made international headlines when he signed with Los Angeles in 2007. Stars like Thierry Henry, David Villa, and Kaká have followed.

English superstar David Beckham was MLS's first designated player when he signed to play with the Los Angeles Galaxy in 2007. He is part of the ownership group for the Miami franchise set to debut in 2019

The world has taken notice, and some US stars who got their start in MLS have signed to play overseas in the world's top leagues. Players like Clint Dempsey, Tim Howard, and Michael Bradley all started in MLS before having successful European careers.

In 2014, an ESPN poll revealed that MLS is equally as popular as Major League Baseball among kids aged 12 to 17. In 2015, MLS signed a new $720 million TV deal with Fox Sports, ESPN, and Univision. 2016 saw an all-time high in average attendance for MLS. Soccer matches are a hot ticket in many MLS markets. Ticket reselling website Ticket IQ reports more than 300 percent growth in the demand for MLS tickets from 2011 to 2017. Most other sports saw less than 10 percent growth.

The continued influx of immigrants from soccer-loving countries has pushed the popularity of the sport forward in America. Mexican soccer gets the highest ratings on American television, and in 2016 a total of more than 36 million viewers watched Premier League matches from England. Although these leagues with a superior quality of play get better viewership than MLS, the level of interest they help to generate helps the sport in all forms in America.

The level of play in MLS, however, continues to improve, and the league continues to grow and provide a **viable** home league for USMNT players. MLS is currently planning a franchise launch in Miami. The ownership group for the new team includes the now-retired Beckham. The Miami franchise is scheduled to debut in 2019. Expansion interest is also coming from cities like Sacramento and Saint Louis.

US Soccer has initiated an audit of the sport
in the country designed to identify ways
to improve talent identification and development

Perhaps the main reason why American soccer is getting better is because of improved coaching and development. More than three million kids play youth soccer in the United States, which is more than any other country in the world. So the talent pool is there; the issue has been finding and developing the potential that exists. In 2017, a Belgian consulting group affiliated with the University of Brussels completed a two-year assessment of US soccer development, a study that was commissioned by the United States Soccer Federation. Auditors specializing in soccer development visited all US Soccer development academies and every MLS club. The Belgian group, called Double PASS, looked at eight critical areas, from talent identification and development to facilities and support staff. Based on this overall assessment, a series of recommended steps will be drawn up for American soccer at various levels. The steps are intended to:

- **create a top-level talent development system and national team environment**
- **produce improved players, national teams, and professional clubs**
- **make the MLS more popular, attractive to top players, and a better business prospect**

In 2013, US Soccer took another progressive step toward the future improvement of the sport domestically. A partnership was set up with the French Football Federation for MLS coaches and academy directors to train for an Elite Formation Coaching License. The idea was to push coaches to honestly assess where they stood against a top-level development system. Licensing requires 320 hours of on-field and classroom learning in an eight-week span. In the first cycle of instruction, many US coaches passed a final assessment to gain the license, yet many did not. Every academy director in France is required to be licensed, but this is not yet true in the United States. Change will take time.

One of the major hurdles to improving the game is improving the level of coaching. Launching the development academy initiative in 2007 was a huge step for the USSF. Now 152 member clubs are following a US Soccer-required curriculum designed to develop technical ability. But this kind of program cannot succeed without top-level coaching. Soccer recruitment is challenged by other opportunities in sport that

SIDEBAR: US SOCCER AGE GROUP COACHING LICENSE RECOMMENDATIONS

Age	U6	U7	U8	U9	U10	U11	U12
Development Stage	Initial	Initial	Initial	Basic	Basic	Basic	Basic
Coaching License Level	F	F	F	E	E	E	E

Age	U13	U14	U15	U16	U17	U18	U19
Development Stage	Intermediate	Intermediate	Advanced	Advanced	Advanced	Advanced	Specific
Coaching License Level	D	D	C + B	C + B	C + B	C + B	A

Source: US Soccer

US Soccer has partnered with the French Football Federation to have high level US coaches measure themselves against a top-flight development system

good athletes have in America versus the rest of the world. In addition, soccer is underfunded in the United States compared to other sports, but especially compared to its European counterpart.

This is why coaches need to know how to recognize talent and how to encourage and develop it within the sport. Player development can only go as far as the quality of the coach doing the developing can take it. In other improvement efforts, US Soccer coach licensing was revamped in 2015. There are now new, tougher requirements for A-, B-, and C-level licenses (high to low). The aforementioned MLS and the academy director licenses are offered by invitation only, but in the future, US Soccer hopes to move to an application-based system for these top levels. US Soccer is also planning for continuing education experiences for licensed coaches in the future so that they continue to get better.

US Soccer revamped its licensing system with the future goal to have coaches with appropriate levels of knowledge and experience at all levels of the sport nationwide

All in all, the goal is to improve the experience for youth players to make them more skilled and to foster a love for the sport. New rule changes launched in August 2017 are designed to do just that: small-sided games were introduced, with the idea being that kids get more touches of the ball, making the whole game experience more valuable to them. For example, kids aged 7 and under play four-on-four, ages 9 and under play seven-on-seven, and ages 11 and under play nine-on-nine.

All of these changes are being made in pursuit of US Soccer's single-minded goal to have a strong foundation from which to build an American soccer identity that is **coherent** and focused. The push is on to improve the quality of Team USA, and the sport overall, in a country that is really starting to embrace it at its highest level.

TEXT-DEPENDENT QUESTIONS:

1. Which country did the USA defeat to qualify for the 1990 World Cup?

2. Which famous player is a member of the ownership group for the MLS team proposed to begin play in Miami in 2019?

3. What are the three different configurations for small-sided matches?

RESEARCH PROJECT:

Which players will be the faces of the USMNT in the future? Do some research on players for the under-17 national team. Choose two and create player profiles using photos, videos and statistics for each, including their vital soccer information as well as interesting facts about where, why, and how they learned to play the game.

Advantage: when a player is fouled but play is allowed to continue because the team that suffered the foul is in a better position than they would have been had the referee stopped the game.

Armband: removable colored band worn around the upper arm by a team's captain, to signify that role.

Bend: skill attribute in which players strike the ball in a manner that applies spin, resulting in the flight of the ball curving, or bending, in mid-air.

Bicycle kick: a specific scoring attempt made by a player with their back to the goal. The player throws their body into the air, makes a shearing movement with the legs to get one leg in front of the other, and attempts to play the ball backwards over their own head, all before returning to the ground. Also known as an *overhead kick*.

Box: common name for the penalty area, a rectangular area measuring 44 yards (40.2 meters) by 18 yards (16.5 meters) in front of each goal. Fouls occurring within this area result in a penalty kick.

Club: collective name for a team, and the organization that runs it.

CONCACAF: acronym for the *Confederation of North, Central American and Caribbean Association Football*, the governing body of the sport in North and Central America and the Caribbean; pronounced "kon-ka-kaff."

CONMEBOL: acronym for the South American Football Association, the governing body of the sport in South America; pronounced "kon-me-bol."

Corner kick: kick taken from within a 1-yard radius of the corner flag; a method of restarting play when a player plays the ball over their own goal line without a goal being scored.

Cross: delivery of the ball into the penalty area by the attacking team, usually from the area between the penalty box and the touchline.

Dead ball: situation when the game is restarted with the ball stationary; i.e., a free kick.

Defender: one of the four main positions in soccer. Defenders are positioned in front of the goalkeeper and have the principal role of keeping the opposition away from their goal.

Dribbling: when a player runs with the ball at their feet under close control.

Flag: small rectangular flag attached to a handle, used by an assistant referee to signal that they have seen a foul or other infraction take place. "The flag is up" is a common expression for when the assistant referee has signaled for an offside.

Flick-on: when a player receives a pass from a teammate and, instead of controlling it, touches the ball with their head or foot while it is moving past them, with the intent of helping the ball reach another teammate.

Forward: one of the four main positions in football. Strikers are the players closest to the opposition goal, with the principal role of scoring goals. Also known as a *striker* or *attacker*.

Free kick: the result of a foul outside the penalty area given against the offending team. Free kicks can be either direct (shot straight toward the goal) or indirect (the ball must touch another player before a goal can be scored).

Fullback: position on either side of the defense, whose job is to try to prevent the opposing team attacking down the wings.

Full-time: the end of the game, signaled by the referees whistle. Also known as the *final whistle*.

Goal difference: net difference between goals scored and goals conceded. Used to differentiate league or group stage positions when clubs are tied on points.

Goalkeeper: one of the four main positions in soccer. This is the player closest to the goal a team is defending. They are the only player on the pitch that can handle the ball in open play, although they can only do so in the penalty area.

Goal kick: method of restarting play when the ball is played over the goal line by a player of the attacking team without a goal being scored.

Goal-line technology: video replay or sensor technology systems used to determine whether the ball has crossed the line for a goal or not.

Hat trick: when a player scores three goals in a single match.

Header: using the head as a means of playing or controlling the ball.

Linesman: another term for the assistant referee that patrols the sideline with a flag monitoring play for fouls, offsides, and out of bounds.

Long ball: attempt to distribute the ball a long distance down the field without the intention to pass it to the feet of the receiving player.

Manager: the individual in charge of the day-to-day running of the team. Duties of the manager usually include overseeing training sessions, designing tactical plays, choosing the team's formation, picking the starting eleven, and making tactical switches and substitutions during games.

Man of the Match: an award, often decided by pundits or sponsors, given to the best player in a game.

Midfielder: one of the four main positions in soccer. Midfielders are positioned between the defenders and forwards.

OFC: initials for the *Oceania Football Confederation*, the governing body of the sport in Oceania.

Offside: a player is offside if they are in their opponent's half of the field and closer to the goal line than both the second-last defender and the ball at the moment the ball is played to them by a teammate. Play is stopped and a free kick is given against the offending team.

Offside trap: defensive tactical maneuver, in which each member of a team's defense will simultaneously step forward as the ball is played forward to an opponent, in an attempt to put that opponent in an offside position.

Own goal: where a player scores a goal against their own team, usually as the result of an error.

Penalty area: rectangular area measuring 44 yards (40.2 meters) by 18 yards (16.5 meters) in front of each goal; commonly called *the box*.

Penalty kick: kick taken 12 yards (11 meters) from goal, awarded when a team commits a foul inside its own penalty area.

Penalty shootout: method of deciding a match in a knockout competition, which has ended in a draw after full-time and extra-time. Players from each side take turns to attempt to score a penalty kick against the opposition goalkeeper. Sudden death is introduced if scores are level after each side has taken five penalties.

Red card: awarded to a player for either a single serious cautionable offence or following two yellow cards. The player receiving the red card is compelled to leave the game for the rest of its duration, and that player's team is not allowed to replace him with another player. A player receiving the red card is said to have been *sent off* or *ejected*.

Side: another word for team.

Stoppage time: an additional number of minutes at the end of each half, determined by the match officials, to compensate for time lost during the game. Informally known by various names, including *injury time* and *added time*.

Striker: see Forward.

Studs: small points on the underside of a player's boots to help prevent slipping. A tackle in which a player directs their studs toward an opponent is referred to as a *studs-up challenge*, and is a foul punishable by a red card.

Substitute: a player who is brought on to the pitch during a match in exchange for a player currently in the game.

Sweeper: defender whose role is to protect the space between the goalkeeper and the rest of the defense.

Tackle: method of a player winning the ball back from an opponent, achieved either by using the feet to take possession from the opponent, or making a slide tackle to knock the ball away. A tackle in which the opposing player is kicked before the ball is punishable by either a free kick or penalty kick. Dangerous tackles may also result in a yellow or red card.

Throw-in: method of restarting play. Involves a player throwing the ball from behind a touch line after an opponent has kicked it out.

Trap: skill performed by a player, whereupon the player uses their foot (or, less commonly, their chest or thigh) to bring an airborne or falling ball under control.

UEFA: acronym for *Union of European Football Associations*, the governing body of the sport in Europe; pronounced "you-eh-fa."

Winger: wide midfield player whose primary focus is to provide crosses into the penalty area. Alternatively known as a *wide midfielder*.

World Cup: commonly refers to the men's FIFA World Cup tournament held every four years, but is also associated with the FIFA Women's World Cup, international tournaments for youth football, (such as the FIFA U-20 World Cup), and the FIFA Club World Cup.

Yellow card: shown by the referee to a player who commits a cautionable offence. If a player commits two cautionable offences in a match, they are shown a second yellow card, followed by a red card, and are then sent off. Also known as a *caution* or a *booking*.

FURTHER READING, INTERNET RESOURCES & VIDEO CREDITS:

Further Reading:

Clemente, A. Lisi. *A History of the U.S. Men's National Soccer Team.* Lanham, MD: Rowman & Littlefield Publishers, 2017.

West, Phil. *The United States of Soccer: MLS and the Rise of American Soccer Fandom.* New York, NY: The Overlook Press, 2016.

Jökulssonm, Illugi. *U.S. Men's Team: New Stars on the Field (World Soccer Legends).* New York, NY: Abbeville Kids, 2014.

Internet Resources:

FIFA: www.fifa.com

US Soccer: www.ussoccer.com

Major League Soccer: www.mlssoccer.com

Video Credits:

Chapter 1:
Check out the highlights from the USMNT win over Colombia at the 1994 World Cup
http://x-qr.net/1Fwu

Chapter 2:
Watch highlights from the 2002 World Cup quarterfinals against Germany
http://x-qr.net/1GbD

Chapter 3:
Check out this career retrospective of Landon Donovan
http://x-qr.net/1DLg

Chapter 4:
Michael Bradley steals and stuns with a brilliant goal against Mexico
http://x-qr.net/1EnH

Chapter 5:
The largest crowd ever for an MLS Cup final was in New England in 2002
http://x-qr.net/1FZL

INDEX

INDEX

Andrew Luke

ABOUT THE AUTHOR:

Andrew Luke is a former journalist, reporting on both sports and general news for many years at television stations in various locations across the US affiliated with NBC, CBS and Fox. Prior to his journalism career he worked with the Boston Red Sox Major League baseball team. An avid writer and sports enthusiast, he has authored 26 other books on sports topics. In his downtime Andrew enjoys family time with his wife and two young children and attending hockey and baseball games in his home city of Pittsburgh, PA.

PICTURE CREDITS: